To:

From:

Bah Humbug!

AND EVERYTHING ELSE
WE LOVE ABOUT CHRISTMAS

MICHAEL W. DOMIS

ILLUSTRATED BY BONNIE KREBS

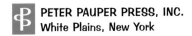

PETER PAUPER PRESS, INC.
White Plains, New York

To Jesus—the birthday boy
MWD

Illustrations copyright © 2005 Bonnie Krebs
Designed by Heather Zschock

Copyright © 2005
Peter Pauper Press, Inc.
202 Mamaroneck Avenue
White Plains, NY 10601
All rights reserved
ISBN 1-59359-992-7
Printed in China
7 6 5 4 3 2 1

BaH HuMbuG!

AND EVERYTHING ELSE
WE LOVE ABOUT CHRISTMAS

Introduction

Christmas is a time of joy, peace, harmony, laughter, and love, celebrated by calling one's relatives together to bask in the contented glow of familial bliss. I think we can all agree that's what Christmas is *billed* as.

But for all its joy, peace, harmony, and love, the Christmas season can take its toll. After month four of preparing for the Big Red Day, *Exit Stage Left* Spirit of Giving, *Enter Stage Right* Ebenezer Scrooge! Any adult who has seen enough Christmases past knows just how crippling this malady can be.

Christmas was once a lovely slow-down period in our lives—a peaceful time to reflect on the previous year, to share memories, news, hopes, and dreams with those near and dear to us. Nowadays it's beginning to look a lot like Christmas, and it's only the 4th of July! By mid-November, we're wishing the First Noel were the Last. The season's stress brings out the Humbug in us, no matter how much joy we struggle to bring to the world.

This book is for the Humbug in all of us. Perhaps laughing at the season's hassles will help take some of the **NO!** out of NOEL, and this little book will serve as a potent painkiller for all manner of Christmas headaches. It may help us avoid dipping into the eggnog in October and keep us away from the pharmacy counter in November.

What follows are words of wisdom from curmudgeons of Christmas past and present, and our observations on the 12 Humbugs of Christmas (only 12!), appearing, of course, in their holiday best.

CHRISTMAS CURMUDGEON CORNER

"If I had my way, everyone who went around with 'Merry Christmas' on their lips would be boiled in their own pudding and buried with a stake of holly through their heart."

Ebenezer Scrooge in *A Christmas Carol*
by Charles Dickens

The 12 Humbugs of Christmas

On the first day of Christmas, this Humbug came to me:

BUYING A TREE

This has become an annual quest. Not an errand that one does joyfully and with a light heart, but a quest. A quest of mythic proportions, so that with the cry of "Let's go get a tree!" the stomach starts churning out acid by the gallon in anticipation of the endless hours spent in polar surrounds searching for the "perfect" tree.

It begins at the local Home and Garden Emporium in Quadrangle E, just below Section C, located, naturally, on the windward side of the premises, perched on a cliff. As a brisk 45 mph wind lightly ruffles your collar and every hair on your face takes on the appearance of iced barbed wire, you stare blankly at acres of projectiles dressed fetchingly in festive red fishnet stockings. You want to cry. But you dare not, for if

you cry, your eyelids will surely freeze shut and your eyelashes snap off at the roots like little baby icicles.

Now your spouse asks you to un-net and "fluff" the tree she's pointing at. Because you know that finding a salesperson to assist you is almost as difficult as finding the right tree itself, you produce the retractable knife you purchased for just such a purpose and begin cutting the net off. Immediately a gaggle of salespeople shows up to castigate you for doing their job. One of them expertly unzips the tree, fluffs the branches, spins it, and holds it for inspection while your

spouse eyes it critically.

"Not quite," your spouse says, "there's a bald spot near the base. We'll keep looking, thank you."

Before you can tell the salesperson to stick around, he's thanked your spouse and disappeared along with his sensibly parka-clad cohorts, never to be seen again.

Now it's *your* job to un-net, fluff, spin, and present the next 324 trees. When you have finally finished with #324, your spouse puts a thoughtful finger to her chin and says, "You know, I think I can live with that little bald spot. Let's get the first one we saw, okay?"

With gritted teeth, you drag the chosen tree the mile and a half to the checkout only to discover that you have selected the only tree on the lot without a price code, necessitating the infamous "PRICE CHECK ON 16!" A runner is dispatched to the designated quadrant

and reappears 20 minutes later, breathlessly to report the same figure you'd already given the cashier.

After you pay for your tree, you drag it to the parking lot where someone who is just waiting to be tipped re-nets the tree in netting that's guaranteed to break every instrument you possess for cutting (except for a diamond saw, which you don't own, but can rent from the same home and garden store for $50 an hour). But you don't discover this until you are at your home, 20 miles away.

CHRISTMAS CURMUDGEON CORNER

There are some people who want
to throw their arms around you simply
because it is Christmas; there are
other people who want to strangle
you simply because it is Christmas.

Robert Lynd

On the second day of Christmas, this Humbug came to me:

DECORATING THE TREE

*g*ood, you brought the tree home and de-netted it. You've even managed to mount it in the stand without causing major damage to your home, the tree, your spouse, or children. Now, comes the decorating part. Isn't this fun? Isn't it?

You will now spend four hours untangling and straightening the Christmas tree lights. Then you must test the lights. Each of the 45 strands your spouse wants strung on the tree has at least one burned-out bulb—which everybody knows, and contrary to the printed insert in the package, causes at least half the strand not to light, or causes it to blink intermittently. You don't have any spare bulbs. Off to the

store you go. Oh no, the store doesn't carry the replacement bulbs any more. So you buy 45 strands of the new European designer Christmas lights, hoping your spouse will like them. Your spouse adores them. Hooray for you.

What's wrong? Why won't they light? Aha!—those pesky European strands require a 220-volt converter. Back to the store. Home again, you assemble the array of switches and wires with the precision of a master lighting technician preparing for a pop concert. Flipping the master switch to "on," you are struck blind: 2,000 little light bulbs at 220 volts is *bright*—and

hot. When your vision clears, you notice that the cat has burst into flames. You grab the flaming feline, rush outside and stuff it into a snowbank. Although unhurt, your pet now resembles Mr. Bigglesworth from *Austin Powers*.

On your way back inside, you hear a strange whizzing sound. It's your electric meter. You are now consuming more electricity per hour than Guam.

You point this out to your spouse, who is stumbling around groping for the switch. Your spouse agrees that maybe cutting back to ten strands of lights might be a good idea.

Now it becomes your sole purpose in life for the next eight hours to be the Ornament Holder and Passer. Carefully unwrap each ornament from its tissue paper cradle, identify it to your spouse, recount

any relevant Family Lore associated with the decoration, and then hand it gently to him or her so that it may be hung on the tree. There are 4,385 ornaments to be hung. Now would be a good time for a quick review of elementary physics—fulcrums, centers of gravity, and the like. Do it now, before the tree falls over from being too heavily weighted on one side.

Once the tree is decorated, it is a shining, wondrous spectacle.

It will last exactly two days—until 90 percent of the needles fall off.

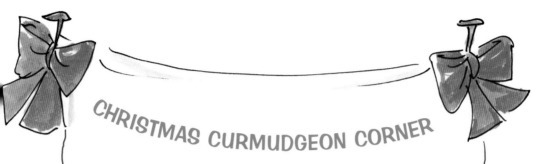

Christmas is a time when
you get homesick—
even when you're home.

Carol Nelson

On the third day of Christmas, this Humbug came to me:

OUTDOOR DECORATING

You forgot (yet again!) to book an outdoor crane to install the blinking, animated reindeer on the roof. You've found gashes the size of your son's toy sword in the inflatable snowman and Santa figures. Your decorative signs directing Santa to the chimney were shanghaied by that same son for the holiday play. The lighted baby Jesus melted in a horrible manger accident last year. You decide to keep it simple ("classic!") and settle for a few strands of Christmas lights. You will mount your icy roof in the dead of winter, most likely in the dark, and hang strands of lights from the eaves.

You try, every year, to hang the same lights. You really do. It's a waste of money to buy new lights each season. But every single time you open that box of lights, no matter how carefully packed from the previous season, you always end up with one large snarled ball of cheer.

I believe, based on absolutely no evidence to the contrary, that Christmas lights mate in the off-season and breed more bulbs. Having discovered your randy bulbs, you have several choices. You can attempt to untangle the lights, which may take until June. Or you can throw the whole mess out, vow to be more careful (like that'll work!), and go out and buy more lights.

Or you could do what I do: just hang the whole mess on the corner of the house and call it an *"objet d'art."*

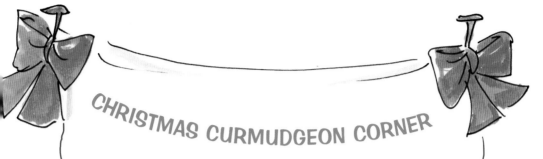

CHRISTMAS CURMUDGEON CORNER

Next to a circus, ain't nothing
that packs up and tears out faster
than the Christmas spirit.

Kin Hubbard

On the fourth day of Christmas, this Humbug came to me:

CATALOGS

Top Ten Things to Do With All Those Christmas Catalogs

10. Construct a life-size papier-mâché manger scene.

9. Stamp them all with: "I'm dead. Return to sender."

8. Glue them to yourself and go as "Christmas Catalog Person" for Halloween. (Worry not; you'll have enough by Halloween to make several costumes.)

7. Save them until Christmas, and construct a life-size replica of the George Washington Bridge. (With the leftover catalogs, you can make Yankee Stadium.)

6. Wrap ten-pound stacks of catalogs in duct tape. When you have enough, build a house.

5. Roll them up very tightly. Use them in the fireplace. You may never have to pay another heating bill!

4. Go downtown and hand them out as "free samples."

3. Package ten-pound stacks in gift wrapped boxes. Give to neighbors. Say they're "homemade."

2. Offer catalogs on eBay as "collector's items."

And the number one thing to do with catalogs is ...

1. Construct a dogsled and run the Iditarod. Extra catalogs can be used to clean up after the dogs.

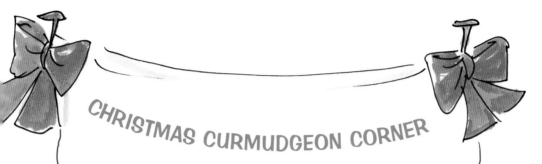

CHRISTMAS CURMUDGEON CORNER

Christmas is a time of joy,
and the way your mother spends,
the storeowners in this
town are ecstatic.

Jack Domis

On the fifth day of Christmas, this Humbug came to me:

CHRISTMAS JOLLYITIS

A public service announcement from the Publisher:

*G*entle reader: is there someone you know who celebrates Christmas just a little too much each year? A relative, perhaps, who begins to talk about getting ready for next Christmas on December 26th? A friend, maybe, who leaves his decorations up, and lit, year-round?

Well, those are just two of the warning signs of Christmas Jollyitis. Christmas Jollyitis is a non-debilitating but highly annoying condition

that causes those not afflicted to avoid at all costs those who are.

There are warning signs, however. We urge you to be aware of them.

Warning Signs of Christmas Jollyitis

Does the afflicted:

1. Begin humming or singing Christmas carols just after Easter?

2. Start wearing Christmas-themed apparel (ties, blouses, sweaters) in February?

3. Start every conversation with, "So, what do you want Santa to bring you this year?"

4. Frequently say, "I just LOVE Christmas, don't you?" without provocation?

5. Argue violently with grocery store personnel over the lack of eggnog in August?

6. Know all the words to "Grandma Got Run Over by a Reindeer"?

7. React violently when told, "You know, there ARE other holidays besides Christmas"?

If you have a friend or loved one afflicted with this annoying condition, take comfort: you are not alone in your suffering.

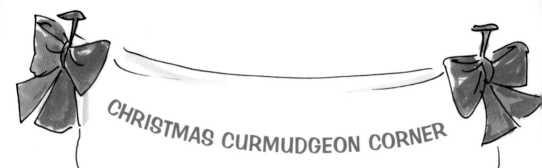

CHRISTMAS CURMUDGEON CORNER

From a commercial point of view,
if Christmas did not exist it
would be necessary to invent it.

Katharine Whitehorn

On the sixth day of Christmas, this Humbug came to me:

GIFT SHOPPING

From the Department of "What Were YOU Thinking?"

O kay, we've all had lapses of taste at one time or another. However . . . some gifts are beyond the pale. Don't let this happen to you, or those you love.

Our top five gifts NOT to give:

5. Clothing for cats. We really shouldn't have to say this, but even for now-naked and shivering Mr. Bigglesworth, cute sweaters and little socks are simply too great an assault on feline dignity. Diminished self-respect in cats can lead to a host of problems, including social isolation (the other cats in the neighborhood will

make fun of him) and litter-box rejection (he will show you exactly what he thinks of your gift . . . on the living room carpet).

4. Technology for the technologically challenged. There is no greater heartbreak than watching your mother try to plug a cell phone into a standard phone jack, or hearing the wail of a relative lamenting that "the Internet is broken." Although it's tempting to want to see Grandpa boogie down with the latest digital music mini-player, you—and he—probably aren't ready. Spare yourself and your family this agony.

3. Camping gear for couch potatoes. Your brother will wind up using that -50° sleeping bag to line the dog's bed, or bivouac the Antarctic-approved tent in the garage. Hiking boots do make handy storage bins for beer cans and the remote, however.

2. A diet book. For anybody. 'Nuff said.

And the number one gift that should **NEVER** be given under any circumstances is ...

1. Fruitcake. Do you know anyone who actually eats fruitcake? We don't either. Do we even know what's in a fruitcake? Do we want to know? Sure, it's fruit, but that doesn't account for the fact that a small fruitcake can weigh more than a brick. Unless you know your relative needs a doorstop, or has a loose paving stone on the front walk, eschew fruitcake. Your family will thank you.

   . . . Oh, and a "This Job Sucks" t-shirt is probably not the best choice of gift for your boss, either.

A quick rant:

Okay, it might not be so bad if retailers didn't think the season began the day after Labor Day. And it wouldn't be so bad if all the retailers charged the same price so you wouldn't have to go from store to store comparing prices, only to finally buy the gift from the one store that doesn't take returns, and then discover the very next day that it's half-price at the store on the corner.

It's enough to make you stick burning sprigs of holly in your eyes.

NO RETURNS!

Ever... Happy Holidays!

YOU
BOUGHT
IT...
YOU
KEEP
IT!

NO
RETURNS
EXCHANGES
NOTHING
DON'T EVEN ASK!

NO NO NO
NO NO NO
RETURNS!

ABSOLUTELY POSITIVELY
NO
RETURNS...NO EXCEPTIONS!

CHRISTMAS CURMUDGEON CORNER

The worst gift is a fruitcake.
There is only one fruitcake in
the entire world, and people keep
sending it to each other.

Johnny Carson

On the seventh day of Christmas, this Humbug came to me:

HANDMADE GIFTS

lame this on you-know-who. Sure, she's paid her debt to society, but her real crime is to have created the insane notion that amateurs, without the aid of an army of assistants, can create aesthetically appealing and truly useful gifts made from brown paper and a pot of decoupage medium. Worse, she's made us believe that the recipients of said homemade gifts will be overjoyed to receive them and awed at our talent. That last part is, of course, a crock of eggnog.

What reaction is usually forthcoming when someone receives a handmade gift for Christmas?

"Oh, how . . . unique."

"Really?" the perpetrator asks, "Do you really like it? I knitted it myself."

"Well, it's a . . . very nice job. I mean, colors like these . . . well . . . they only exist in . . . yarn."

"Oh, that's so sweet of you to say," the clueless crafter gushes on, oblivious to sarcasm. "I was so afraid you wouldn't like it."

"No . . . no. . . ." the victim says through clenched teeth, suffering physical pain from the stress of telling such an outrageous lie, "I do like it. Really, I do. I needed a sweater like this."

"Oh, that is just so great," the knitter continues unabated, "because I knitted you a pair of socks and a pair of underwear, too."

Get the picture, folks? If you are one of these perpetrators of hand-made gifts, and if your name is *not* Martha Stewart, please stop. We

don't want to have to keep lying to you.

And if you know someone who's planning to make gifts this year, make it your business to remember: "Friends don't let friends knit underwear for Christmas gifts."

Aunt flo, the socks and fruitcake are just perfect. But I want you to know that I wouldn't be offended if you gave me a gift certificate next year.

Nicole Beale

On the eighth day of Christmas, this Humbug came to me:

CHRISTMAS CARDS

I think only women who have been trained by their mothers for generations *ad infinitum* can actually write and send Christmas cards. I have absolutely no sense of it. Sure, I've seen my mother do it. She takes out her address book, looks at some kind of arcane coding next to each name, and decides that this year, she's sending out only 340 cards instead of the usual 350 cards because 10 people didn't acknowledge her card by sending one back last year. After addressing 340 cards, she invariably discovers that she has about 10 left over. So she sends them to the people she was cursing only eight hours before when she began this process.

Christmas cards also come with their own accessories: special Christmas stamps, little holiday stickers, return labels, and fancy glitter pens. Don't insult my mother by affixing an ordinary, everyday stamp on the envelope or using a plain ballpoint pen. She will slash you off her list so fast you won't believe it. She has a higher standard than even Santa for the "naughty and nice" list.

And can we discuss the "family letters" that we receive from people? I am convinced that the only reason people compose these things is to bludgeon others with the good fortunes of the sender. Once, just once, I'd like to get a family letter like the following:

"It's been a crummy year here at the Smiths'. Grandpa developed some kind of rash that requires daily brushing with a scrivener's thistle. Grandma was arrested for running a numbers racket out of the basement. The children have all become members of a religious cult.

They sold off all their belongings—ours too—and moved to a communal farm in Tuscaloosa. So we're living in a big, empty house. But on the bright side, Bob wasn't indicted for embezzlement until *after* Thanksgiving, and we think he can cop a plea. We'll probably have him with us for a couple of months before they send him to the Big House. I feel just fine about all this—the antidepressants seem to be working. Happy holidays!

Now, *that's* entertainment.

CHRISTMAS CURMUDGEON CORNER

Christmas begins about the
first of December with an office
party and ends when you finally
realize what you spent, around
April 15th of the next year.

P. J. O'Rourke

On the ninth day of Christmas, this Humbug came to me:

WRAPPING GIFTS

Who exactly was it that decided that gifts needed to be wrapped? In my opinion, it had to be a woman. Guys don't care if the gift is wrapped. It's just one more step to go through to find out what you got. Guys would be perfectly happy if you just handed them the gift.

"Here, Bob. Have a Christmas gift."

"Oh, cool. A tool for destroying things. I've always wanted one of these. Thanks."

Women, however, *love* getting wrapped presents. I've even heard one woman comment to another, "I'd like to open that gift, but the wrapping is just too pretty. I don't want to ruin it."

Children love getting wrapped presents as well. For kids, a great part of the joy of Christmas is ripping the paper off the gift.

But kids don't wrap gifts—and women already know how to wrap gifts.

Therefore, what follows is a short guide for guys on how to wrap Christmas gifts for the people in your lives.

Step 1: If the gift is not in a box, you must place it in a box. Find a box that is just big enough for your gift to fit in. *Do not* place a small gift in a huge box. You may think your woman will find it funny, but she won't. Also, *do not* place a small gift in a series of larger boxes until you've got 15 boxes nested inside one another. Again, she won't think it's funny. Trust me on this. I've done both and even though the wrapped gift was diamonds each time, I still got in trouble because she was so annoyed at opening the gift.

Step 2: Find some appropriate gift wrap for the box. *Do not* under any circumstances use the comics section for *any* gift. Use real wrapping paper with a Christmas theme.

WARNING: The following colors are *not* Christmas colors: pink, black, orange, yellow, purple, or brown. That leaves RED or GREEN. Use those.

Also, beware of any pictures that might be on the wrapping paper. Bunnies, birthday candles, caps and gowns, wedding bells, racing cars, or dinosaurs are not appropriate themes for wrapping Christmas gifts.

Step 3: Procure tape and ribbon and bow. Follow the above color guidelines for the ribbon and bow. In this situation, duct tape is not acceptable. Now I know you have to use duct tape somewhere in this project. I suggest that instead of using it on the outside, you use it to close the box. That way you'll have satisfied your need to use duct

tape, and she won't see it until later. On the outside, you must use clear cellophane or invisible tape. *Do not* use packing tape. Anything over three-quarters of an inch is just too wide, okay?

Now that we've established the basics, we can safely skip the technical aspects of wrapping the gift. Although you may be tempted to use your laser-guided measuring stick, diamond matrix plotter, and industrial vise to make use of your own gifts from Christmases past, trust me, the tools—while making you feel manly—will be more trouble than they're worth.

You've spent three hours on your wrap job. Now fast forward to the fun part: when she opens the gift.

WHAT?? You didn't remove the price tag?

(Time for a several-beer break.)

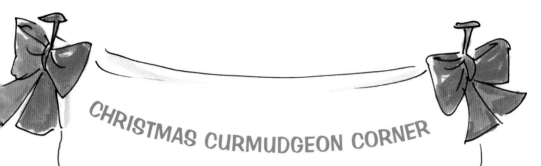

CHRISTMAS CURMUDGEON CORNER

Nothing's as mean as giving

a little child something

useful for Christmas.

Kin Hubbard

On the tenth day of Christmas, this Humbug came to me:

VISITING RELATIVES

Christmas seems to be a convenient excuse to invite over to your house all of the relations you've been avoiding for the other 364 days (and often with good reason, I might add). Or maybe you and your clan descend on the home of another.

Nothing destroys a holiday quite like a protracted family get-together. We're all so close and cuddly, we've mastered all the ins and outs of really getting on each other's nerves.

Invariably there's at least one relative who has some kind of issue that no one cares to discuss.

"What's wrong with Uncle Jim?"

"Well, he hasn't been quite right since, well, you know."

"Since when?"

"Since (always whispered) the accident."

"Oh."

You're no closer to knowing than when you first asked, but don't bother digging anymore. Nobody really wants to face the truth about Uncle Jim anyway. So why not go talk to your "weird" aunt or cousin? The profile varies, but everybody's got one. It might be the aunt who doesn't quite get the concept that you're no longer in second grade, and haven't been for several decades. Or the cousin who gave up on remembering people's names and refers to all the women by their hair color. Or the symptom-maniac who cheerfully regales the holiday

table with tales of his biopsy.

Christmas is a time to reflect on the true blessing of family—the blessing that you need interact with these people only once a year.

CHRISTMAS CURMUDGEON CORNER

Santa Claus has the right idea—
visit people once a year.

Victor Borge

On the eleventh day of Christmas, this Humbug came to me:

BAKING

I t's 9 o'clock. You're tucking your freshly scrubbed child into bed, because tomorrow's a school day. Your child looks at you loving-ly and says those unforgettable words: "Uh, Mom?"

Now, your guard's up, because nothing good ever begins with that phrase.

"Yes, dear?"

"I promised the teacher that you'd make cookies for the class holiday party."

"I'm sure we can take care of that," you respond, idly. "When's the party?"

"Tomorrow," your progeny says.

"Tomorrow?" you scream. "How long have you known about this?"

"Since two weeks," the child answers.

"Why didn't you tell me two weeks ago?" you ask, knowing full well what's coming.

"I forgot," he/she/it says.

You quell the urge to throttle your child and get up quietly, but you don't make it to the door before the dreaded, "Uh, mom?"

"What?" through clenched teeth.

"Can you make them in dreidel shapes with sparkles and blue icing? I promised."

Now, as every mother knows, whatever you need to make cookies at this time of night is *not* in your kitchen.

You check the flour, only to remember that you used the last of it to make a volcano for a school project.

Because of yesterday's impromptu juggling performance involving your now-naked cat and your child, you're out of eggs.

In a fit of middle-aged pique and in an effort to jump-start a low-fat diet, your husband has tossed out every stick of butter and margarine. All you can find is a container of faux margarine whose label reads, "Do not use for cooking."

Your teenage daughter has declared war on sugar. It's all gone, except for four packages of artificial sweetener. Not enough.

At the grocery store, you encounter 40 other parents wandering

around the baking aisle desperately trying to remember what goes into sugar cookies.

Of course, you can't just buy bakery cookies and pass them off as homemade. Not because you're above that sort of thing, but, because every other parent thought of it first, the store is sold out. And try as you might, you just can't figure out how to convince anyone that you can bake cookies that look exactly like Oreos.

Back in the baking aisle, you grab the last five-pound bag of sugar, and look for the flour. The only thing left is rice flour. You take it.

You wind up in an altercation in the dairy case over the last carton of eggs. You are ashamed that you called the PTA president a "poopy head," but at least you got the eggs.

Six hours later, as you are packing the cookies into a decorative tin,

your child wanders downstairs and turns on the radio.

"It looks like lots of kids are gonna be really happy. It's the last day of school before Christmas break, and we've got six inches of the white stuff on the ground! School's been canceled!"

"Mom, what's for breakfast?"

You slump to the floor. "Cookies," you reply.

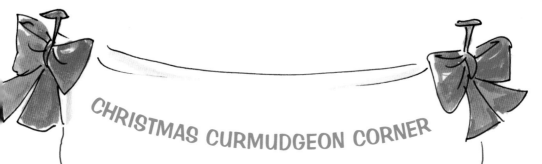

CHRISTMAS CURMUDGEON CORNER

What I don't like about office
Christmas parties is having to look
for another job the next day.

Phyllis Diller

On the twelfth day of Christmas, this Humbug came to me:

PUTTING THE TOY TOGETHER

It's 10 o'clock on Christmas Eve. The children are finally asleep, having consumed five gallons of eggnog and 17 candy canes each. They are vibrating lightly, but asleep nonetheless.

You settle down to watch your favorite Christmas movie, which has been playing 24/7 since All Saints' Day, when your spouse announces: "We have to put together the toy we bought the kids, remember?"

You retrieve the toy, open the box, pull

out the instructions and begin reading: "Warning: Opening the box without first calling 888-MIRACLE-TOY and entering the special 184-digit code found on the aventricular side of the box will void your warranty." Code? you think. Aventricular? you ponder.

No matter, you'll put the toy together so it won't break. Let's see, tools required . . . one spandgler . . . a left handed froom . . . an inna-gaddadavida. Hmmm . . . you don't seem to have these tools. Let's read on: "The spandgler is a special tool that is required by law to insert the flavion into the medjule. We know it looks like a Phillips head screwdriver, but we assure you we have constructed these screws so that only *our* spandgler will really work on them. Spandglers can be purchased online at www.miracletoys/youreupacreek.com or by calling 888-MIRACLE-TOY between the hours

of 11:30 AM and 11:45 AM Merovingian time where our dedicated customer service representatives will be happy to irritate you by pretending to barely speak English."

Halfway through the process of putting the toy together, you pause for a moment and notice that it's now 3 AM. You know the children will awaken in at most, two hours, so you forgo your restroom break and return to work.

At 4 AM it dawns on you that you're running out of parts faster than you're running out of instructions. You panic and quickly flip pages to discover what parts you might be missing. It turns out that you're not missing any parts; it's only that the manual is written in several different languages including Cantonese,

Czech, and Basque. You wonder for a moment if there are any Basque fathers trying to do what you're trying to do. Wonder what the curse words are in Czech. You put those thoughts aside and get back to work.

It's 4:30 AM. The end is in sight. One more bleemish to frangle and you're home free. You line up the bleemish, rear back with your floom, and promptly smash the heck out of your thumb.

Your scream wakes up your wife who had fallen asleep on the couch.

Unfortunately, it also wakes up the children who hurtle downstairs like Christmas missiles. You tap the last bleemish into place, slam your tools back into their holders and assume a position of fatherly innocence on the couch while sucking your sore thumb.

You beam with pride as your children goggle at the magnificent

gift you have just spent the whole night assembling. You step into the kitchen to prepare coffee while the kids finish demolishing the wrapping on the other gifts.

Whilst sipping your coffee, you notice the children race by you excitedly on their way outside.

You look into the living room. The gift you have put together is still there.

Puzzled, you look outside to behold your children, laughing and playing with the box.

CHRISTMAS CURMUDGEON CORNER

"A Merry Christmas, uncle!
God save you!" cried a cheerful voice.

"Bah!" said Scrooge. "Humbug!"

A Christmas Carol, by Charles Dickens